TEC

2/08

D1733112

Powerful Predators

POLAR BEARS
ARCTIC HUNTERS

Norman Pearl

PowerKiDS
press
New York

Published in 2009 by The Rosen Publishing Group, Inc.
29 East 21st Street, New York, NY 10010

First Edition

Editor: Amelie von Zumbusch
Book Design: Julio Gil
Photo Researcher: Jessica Gerweck

Photo Credits: Cover, pp. 5, 7, 9, 11, 19 Shutterstock.com; p. 13 © Norbert Rosing/Getty Images; p. 15 © Wayne R. Bilenduke/Getty Images; p. 17 © Ralph Lee Hopkins/Getty Images; p. 21 © Paul Nicklen/Getty Images; back cover (top to bottom) Shutterstock.com, Shutterstock.com, © Kim Wolhuter/Getty Images, Shutterstock.com, © Stephen Frink/Getty Images, Shutterstock.com.

Library of Congress Cataloging-in-Publication Data

Pearl, Norman.
  Polar bears : Arctic hunters / Norman Pearl. — 1st ed.
      p. cm. — (Powerful predators)
  Includes index.
  ISBN 978-1-4042-4510-5 (library binding)
  1. Polar bear—Juvenile literature. I. Title.
  QL737.C27P368 2009
  599.786—dc22
                                            2008010035

Manufactured in the United States of America

Contents

What a Bear!

Good swimmers can do lots of laps in a pool. There are even some swimmers who can swim over 60 miles (97 km) in icy water without stopping! If you think most people cannot swim that far, you are right. These swimmers are polar bears.

Polar bears are among the largest predators, or hunters, on Earth. They see well beneath the water and can spot food as far as 15 feet (5 m) away. Polar bears also have a great sense of **smell**. They can smell food 20 miles (32 km) away. You would not want to be a polar bear's **prey**!

Polar bears are excellent swimmers. In fact, the polar bear's scientific name, *Ursus maritimus*, means "sea bear."

An Icy Home

Most kids will never come across a polar bear on their way to school. These animals live in the Arctic, near the North Pole. Parts of Russia, Norway, Greenland, Canada, and Alaska are in the Arctic. Polar bears are found in all these places.

Polar bears are often spotted along the Arctic coast and on **ice floes**. The bears do not mind the cold **temperatures** there the way people would. In the winter, the average temperature is -29° F (-34° C). During the summer, it warms up to an average temperature of 32° F (0° C). However, that is still **freezing**!

This polar bear is walking across the snow in Churchill, Canada.
Churchill is known for being home to many polar bears.

Hey, Good Looking!

Standing up, a big **male** polar bear can be up to 11 feet (3 m) tall. Large male polar bears weigh about 1,800 pounds (816 kg). This is about as much as four fully-grown male lions! **Female** polar bears are generally less than half this size.

All polar bears have thick fur that helps them keep warm. People often think polar bears are white. However, a polar bear's skin is black, and its fur is made up of clear, hollow hairs. Sunlight reflects, or shines back, from the clear hairs. This makes them look white, in the same way that reflected sunlight makes clear snowflakes look white.

You can see this polar bear's black skin on its nose. A polar bear's nose and footpads are the only parts of the bear's body not covered in fur.

Built for Arctic Life

Polar bears' white-looking coats make them hard to see against the Arctic snow. These bears are made for life in the Arctic! Since much of their food comes from the ocean, these bears are great swimmers. They even have **webbed** feet! A polar bear's feet are useful on land, too. Its large padded paws work like snowshoes on the ice and snow. The bear's paws help it stay warm and keep the bear from slipping.

Polar bears also have another kind of padding to keep out the cold. They have blubber, or fat, under their skin. This blubber keeps polar bears warm and also helps them float in the water.

A polar bear's coat is 1 to 2 inches (2.5–5 cm) thick. Polar bear coats have natural oils that keep them from clumping up when wet.

Here Come the Cubs

Polar bears are used to the Arctic's cold. Unlike most bears, polar bears do not generally spend the winter sleeping in a den. However, female polar bears that have **mated** with a male do dig dens in which to give birth to cubs. Polar bears dig their dens out of the ground or snow. It is about 40° F (22° C) warmer in a polar bear's den than it is outside.

The cubs are born between November and January. At birth, the cubs cannot see or take care of themselves. They weigh less than 2 pounds (1 kg). Newborn polar bear cubs stay very close to their mothers for warmth.

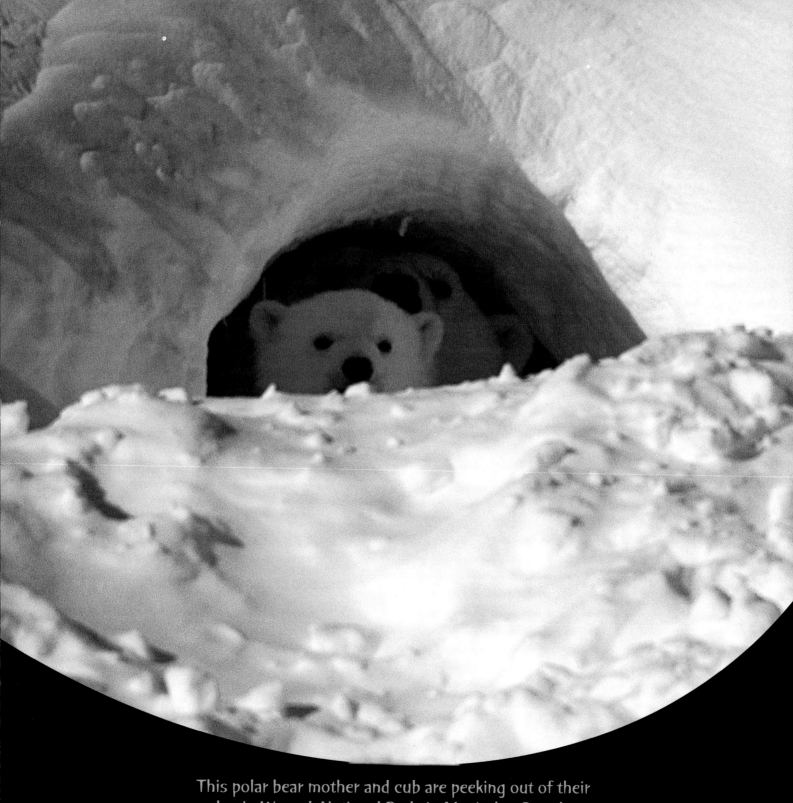

This polar bear mother and cub are peeking out of their den in Wapusk National Park, in Manitoba, Canada.

Growing Up in the Arctic

Newborn polar bear cubs drink their mothers' milk and grow quickly. By the time they are two months old, the cubs start walking inside their dens. In late March or April, they will be ready to go outside.

In the spring, a polar bear mother and her cubs start traveling over the ice to find food. Once their mother kills a seal, cubs have their first solid food. They learn to hunt by watching their mother, but this takes time. Polar bear cubs stay with their mother for about two and a half years before going off on their own.

As all young bears do, polar bear cubs like to play.
They chase each other and climb all over their mothers.

Hungry Hunters

Polar bears spend lots of time hunting. Seals are their favorite prey. Polar bears often wait by a breathing hole or at the edge of the ice. When a seal comes up for air, the polar bear bites into it and pulls it up on the ice. The seal has little chance of getting away.

A polar bear will also creep up on a seal resting on the ice. The bear quickly catches the seal with its long, sharp claws. At times, polar bears attack from the water, too. They swim up to a seal resting on a piece of ice and seize it.

This hungry polar bear is waiting for a seal to come up to breathe.

What's for Supper?

Although the polar bear's favorite food is seals, these bears also eat walruses, reindeer, ducks, and seabirds. Polar bears even eat whales that have beached, or washed up on the coast. Though polar bears are mainly meat eaters, at times they eat eggs, berries, and seaweed, too.

However, polar bears sometimes have trouble finding food. Some young polar bears die of hunger. Quite a few of these beautiful animals never reach their third birthdays. Sometimes, hungry polar bears get into trash left by people. The bears eat whatever food they find there. Sadly, some bears have become very sick and even died after eating trash.

Polar bears can eat more than 150 pounds (68 kg) of meat in one sitting!

Trouble up North

Lately, the number of polar bears has gone down. This has happened for several reasons. For one thing, people have hunted these beautiful animals for sport. **Global warming** has hurt the polar bear, too. As global warming makes the Arctic's ice melt, it becomes harder for the bears to find and hunt seals. Several bears have drowned because they now have to swim much farther between ice floes.

Oil and gas companies have come to places where female bears once built their dens. **Pollutants** from around the world have washed up to the Arctic, as well. All these things mean trouble for the polar bear.

As the amount of ice in the Arctic Ocean grows smaller,
polar bears have fewer and fewer places to hunt and live.

Caring for the Bears

Today, people are taking steps to save the polar bear, but things still do not look good. **Scientists** think we could lose as many as 30 percent of these animals over the next 45 years.

Polar bears live in the United States, Canada, Russia, Greenland, and Norway. At times, the governments in these places have worked together to save polar bears. People are also trying to save the polar bear's **habitat**. More needs to be done, though. Polar bears have been in the Arctic for a long time. We want them to always be there.

Glossary

female (FEE-mayl) Having to do with women and girls.

freezing (FREEZ-ing) The point at which water becomes so cold it turns to ice.

global warming (GLOH-bul WAHRM-ing) A slow increase in how hot Earth is. It is caused by gases that are made when people burn fuels such as gasoline.

habitat (HA-beh-tat) The kind of land where an animal or a plant naturally lives.

ice floes (YS FLOHZ) Large, mostly flat masses of floating ice.

male (MAYL) Having to do with men and boys.

mated (MAYT-ed) Came together to make babies.

pollutants (puh-LOO-tants) Humanmade wastes that hurt Earth's air, land, or water.

prey (PRAY) An animal that is hunted by another animal for food.

scientists (SY-un-tists) People who study the world.

smell (SMEL) To use the nose to find out about something.

temperatures (TEM-pur-cherz) Measures of how hot or cold something is.

webbed (WEBD) Having skin between the toes, as do ducks, frogs, and other animals that swim.

Index

A
animals, 6, 18, 20, 22
Arctic, 6, 10, 20, 22

E
Earth, 4

F
feet, 10
food, 4, 10, 14, 18

G
global warming, 20

H
habitat, 22

I
ice floes, 6, 20

N
North Pole, 6
Norway, 6, 22

P
pollutants, 20
prey, 4, 16

R
Russia, 6, 22

S
scientists, 22
size, 8
swimmers, 4, 10

T
temperature(s), 6

W
water, 4, 10, 16

Web Sites

Due to the changing nature of Internet links, PowerKids Press has developed an online list of Web sites related to the subject of this book. This site is updated regularly. Please use this link to access the list:
www.powerkidslinks.com/pred/polar/